# The Healing Journey for Binge Eating Journal

# Eight Week Journal Companion

*By Michelle Market, LPC, CEDS*

All Rights Reserved.
Copyright © 2014 Michelle C. Market, LPC, CEDS

The Healing Journey for Binge Eating Journal Companion is published by
Michelle Market, LPC, CEDS
First Edition, January 2014

ISBN-13: 978-1494865917

Except as noted, no part of this manual may be reproduced, translated, stored in a retrieval system, or transmitted in any form or by any means, electronic, mechanical, microfilming, or otherwise, without written permission from the Publisher. This manuscript may not be reproduced in part or in whole by any means without the author's expressed permission.

Printed in the United States of America

### Disclaimer

The information in this manual is not intended to provide medical advice and is sold with the understanding that the author is not liable for the misconception or misuse of information provided. This workbook is meant to complement treatment with an eating disorder professional it is **not** intended to replace counseling, therapy or medical treatment. All matters regarding one's health requires medical supervision.

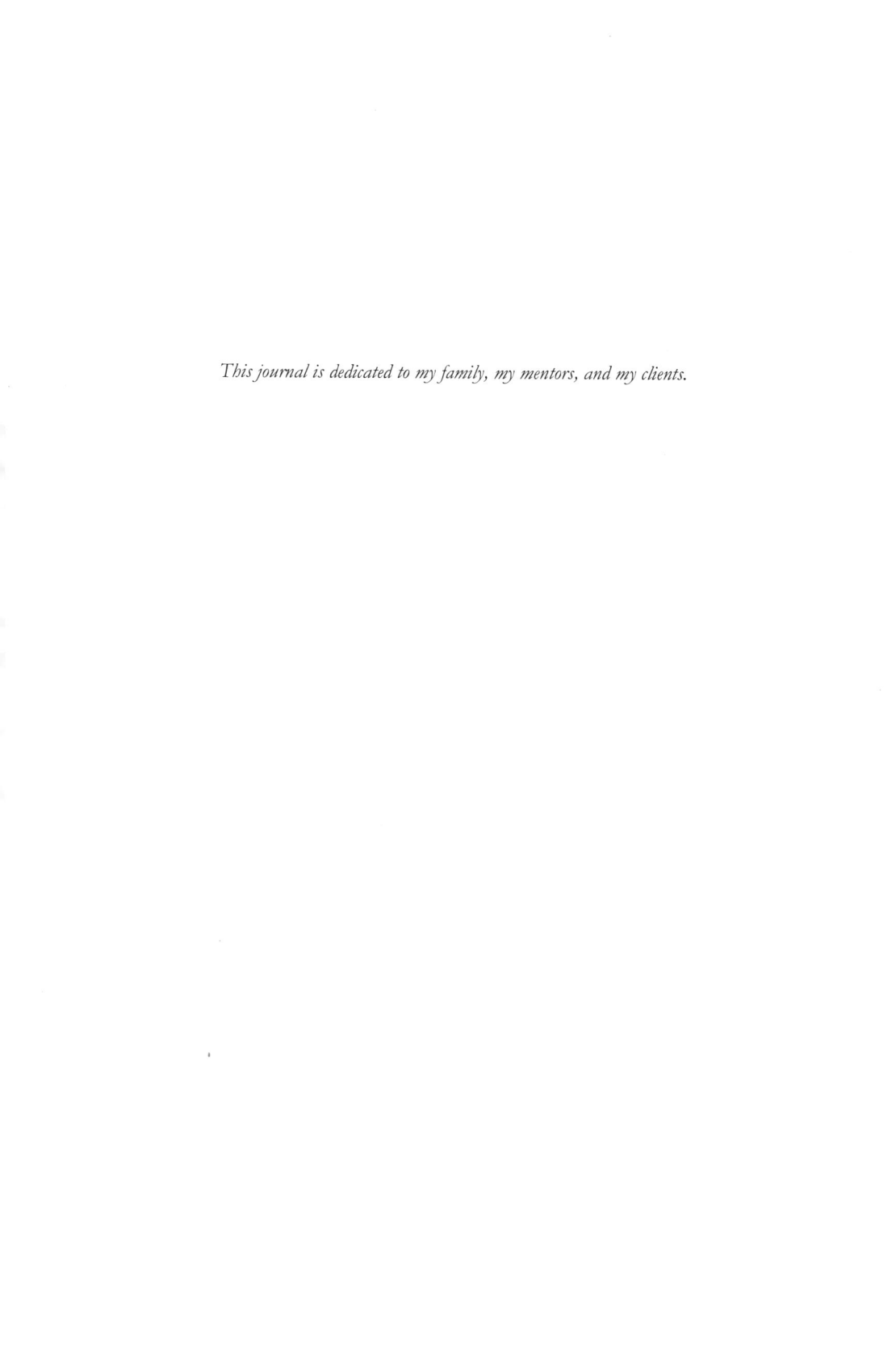

*This journal is dedicated to my family, my mentors, and my clients.*

## *Introduction*

Welcome to the start of your healing journey. It takes a lot of courage and strength to heal, and I want to remind you that you have the resources within you. Over the next eight weeks, I want you to look forward to this time to sit and reflect and spend some quiet time with your thoughts and your feelings.

This companion guide is set up to be used both in the morning for creating a daily intention, and then in the evening for a review of how the day went. Initially this will be difficult to implement, and that is okay. You may find that some days you forget to write in your companion journal, or you may find the task daunting. Just notice those feelings and don't judge them. All those feelings are okay; they are merely information as to what may be going on for that day.

Each week begins with a short lesson, a self-reflection exercise, and a weekly practice. There are fifty-six days of reflections. Each day has a daily reflection, feeling check-in, morning intention, self-compassion reminder, and evening review of the day. At the end of the week, you will notice a weekly review to explore what you noticed during the week with respect to your relationship with food. The appendix is filled with activities that you can incorporate into your journey. Remember, each person's journey is different. You may choose not to write on these pages and instead keep a separate journal to write down your responses. You may even decide not to go in order, and that is okay. The important takeaway of the companion journal is to get into the practice of checking in with yourself, your body, your feelings, and your thoughts on a daily basis. It is that disconnection that perpetuates your binge eating.

Change is not meant to happen overnight. If you are picking up my workbook and companion journal, I suspect that this is not the first time you have tried to heal your relationship with food. I recommend that you go through this journey with a beginner's mind. Act as if you are hearing this information for the first time, even though some of the concepts and encouragements may sound familiar. Please be patient in this journey of healing. You deserve to heal and you can do this. Trust the process and learn to trust yourself.

By no means is fifty-six days a magic number—in fact, I tell all of my clients to give their journey at least one year. Unlike diets, this is not a quick-fix program. In fact, it is just the opposite: The results you gain from your healing journey will last a lifetime.

## Creating Daily Intention

*Choose an item in each category each day, to nourish your mind, body, and spirit.*

| Mind | Body | Spirit |
|---|---|---|
| ☐ Reading | ☐ Eating consistent meals | ☐ Meditating |
| ☐ Writing | ☐ Moving your body | ☐ Praying |
| ☐ Positive affirmations | ☐ Connecting with others | ☐ Having fun |
| ☐ Focusing on other things | ☐ Being grateful for your body | ☐ Reaching out to a friend (having coffee with a friend) |
| ☐ Watching a favorite TV show | ☐ Eating consciously | ☐ Laughing |
| ☐ Talking with others (stimulating discussion) | ☐ Eating without distractions | ☐ Listening to music |
| | ☐ Breathing deeply | ☐ Singing |
| ☐ Learn something new | ☐ Resting | ☐ Reading inspirational writings |
| ☐ Practice mindfulness | ☐ Listening to your body | ☐ Practicing gratitude |
| ☐ Be in the moment | ☐ Stretching your body | ☐ Connecting with nature |
| ☐ Practice self-compassion | | |

*Someone who is addicted to eating is actually starving on an emotional and spiritual level. Her longing for food is a longing for emotional and spiritual nourishment. This is what she is really in pursuit of when she sets out for the grocery store. No matter how much ice cream she eats, how many cookies she consumes, or muffins she devours, she cannot fulfill this longing because she is filling her stomach, not her heart, not her spirit.*
*~ Anita Johnson, <u>Eating in the Light of the Moon</u>*

## Week #1
## Creating Awareness

<u>Lesson</u>:

The first step in changing your relationship with food is becoming aware of your eating patterns. Imagine a relationship with food in which you are using food as nourishment, not for coping. You are eating when you are hungry, stopping when you are full. You are planning your meals instead of making choices based on your environment. You are honoring your needs. It is possible, it just requires patience. It is not about willpower, it is about believing in yourself.

When you turn to food as comfort, most often it is in reaction to something. Preparation is the key to success beginning with knowing what triggers you to eat. The challenge is to determine what you are reacting to when you choose to eat.

What role does food play in your life? Take the following self-assessment to help explore your challenges with food.

- ☐ I think about food all the time
- ☐ After looking through fashion magazines, I feel worse about myself
- ☐ I have dieted most of my life
- ☐ I believe I will be happier when I lose weight
- ☐ When I am on a diet, there are many foods I won't eat because I consider them "bad" or "forbidden" foods.
- ☐ I eat beyond fullness
- ☐ I use food to cope with my feelings
- ☐ I don't feel good about myself
- ☐ I feel my eating is out of control
- ☐ I hide my eating from others
- ☐ I feel ashamed of my eating
- ☐ I am concerned with what others think of me

### Self-Reflection:

What is food replacing in your life? Are you avoiding dealing with disappointment or sadness? Are you in a difficult relationship? Are you unhappy or anxious about life?

_____
_____
_____
_____

### Practice:

Over the course of the week, keep a log of how you are feeling when you are eating. This will provide you with the opportunity to see what drives your eating.

_____
_____
_____
_____
_____
_____
_____
_____
_____
_____
_____
_____
_____
_____
_____
_____
_____
_____
_____

## *Day 1*

### *Acceptance*

*Accept yourself and where you are right now.
As you begin to see yourself in a kinder light, breaking the cycle of self-abuse,
you will slowly and steadily make progress
toward the change that you desire.*

### **Morning Check-In**

How am I feeling? (sad, happy, angry, anxious, overwhelmed, neutral, lonely, hurt).

_____
_____
_____
_____

What am I noticing in my body? (tension, heaviness, lightness, fatigue)

_____
_____
_____
_____

Set an intention for the day (mind/body/spirit)

_____
_____
_____
_____

How will I practice self-compassion? How will I challenge my inner critic? (I choose to support myself, progress not perfection, it is okay to ask for help, I treat myself as a kind and loving friend, one meal at a time.)

_____
_____
_____
_____

## Evening Check-In

What went well today in my healing journey? (I took time for myself. When I ate without distractions, I was able to taste my food. I moved my body). What would I do differently?

_____
_____
_____
_____
_____
_____
_____
_____
_____
_____
_____
_____
_____
_____
_____
_____
_____
_____
_____
_____
_____
_____
_____
_____
_____

*Treat yourself the way you would a cherished friend. You forgive her faults. You tolerate her flaws and mistakes. You cut her lots of slack and you accept her just the way she is, not how you would like her to be. Extend that same kindness, gentleness and understanding to yourself this week.*
*~Stephanie Marston*

## Day 2

### *Awareness*
*Begin to notice your patterns of eating.*
*Do you tend to be hungrier in the morning?*
*Do you eat when you are tired?*
*Do you eat in front of the TV?*

### Morning Check-In

How am I feeling? (sad, happy, angry, anxious, overwhelmed, neutral, lonely, hurt).

_____
_____
_____
_____

What am I noticing in my body? (tension, heaviness, lightness, fatigue)

_____
_____
_____
_____

Set an intention for the day (mind/body/spirit)

_____
_____
_____
_____

How will I practice self-compassion? How will I challenge my inner critic? (I choose to support myself, progress not perfection, it is okay to ask for help, I treat myself as a kind and loving friend, one meal at a time.)

_____
_____
_____
_____

## **Evening Check-In**

What went well today in my healing journey? (I took time for myself. When I ate without distractions, I was able to taste my food. I moved my body). What would I do differently?

_____
_____
_____
_____
_____
_____
_____
_____
_____
_____
_____
_____
_____
_____
_____
_____
_____
_____
_____
_____
_____
_____
_____

*It is good to have an end to journey toward;*
*but it is the journey that matters, in the end.*
*~Ernest Hemingway*

## *Day 3*

### *Choices*
*Create your own healthy choices.
If you are going out for the day, pack a snack bag
so that you can honor your hunger cues
and not feel like a victim of environmental triggers.*

### **Morning Check-In**

How am I feeling? (sad, happy, angry, anxious, overwhelmed, neutral, lonely, hurt).

_____
_____
_____
_____

What am I noticing in my body? (tension, heaviness, lightness, fatigue)

_____
_____
_____
_____

Set an intention for the day (mind/body/spirit)

_____
_____
_____
_____

How will I practice self-compassion? How will I challenge my inner critic? (I choose to support myself, progress not perfection, it is okay to ask for help, I treat myself as a kind and loving friend, one meal at a time.)

_____
_____
_____
_____

## **Evening Check-In**

What went well today in my healing journey? (I took time for myself. When I ate without distractions, I was able to taste my food. I moved my body). What would I do differently?

_____
_____
_____
_____
_____
_____
_____
_____
_____
_____
_____
_____
_____
_____
_____
_____
_____
_____
_____
_____
_____
_____
_____
_____
_____
_____

*The results you achieve will be in
direct proportion to the effort you apply.
~Dennis Waitley*

## *Day 4*

### *Coping*

*How are you feeling right now? Are you sad, lonely, tired, or angry?*
*Begin to take notice of your feelings.*
*It is an important step in changing your relationship with food.*

**Morning Check-In**

How am I feeling? (sad, happy, angry, anxious, overwhelmed, neutral, lonely, hurt).

_____
_____
_____
_____

What am I noticing in my body? (tension, heaviness, lightness, fatigue)

_____
_____
_____
_____

Set an intention for the day (mind/body/spirit)

_____
_____
_____
_____

How will I practice self-compassion? How will I challenge my inner critic? (I choose to support myself, progress not perfection, it is okay to ask for help, I treat myself as a kind and loving friend, one meal at a time.)

_____
_____
_____
_____

### Evening Check-In

What went well today in my healing journey? (I took time for myself. When I ate without distractions, I was able to taste my food. I moved my body). What would I do differently?

_____
_____
_____
_____
_____
_____
_____
_____
_____
_____
_____
_____
_____
_____
_____
_____
_____
_____
_____
_____
_____
_____
_____

*Step confidently forward in precisely the direction that is most challenging to you. Because in that same direction, you'll also find what is most rewarding to you.*
*~Ralph Marston*

## Day 5

### Find Inspiration Along the Way
*Overcoming binge eating is a slow and steady process.*
*Setbacks are learning opportunities.*
*Check in with yourself on a daily basis.*
*Are your goals realistic? Are you trying to take on too much at once?*

### Morning Check-In

How am I feeling? (sad, happy, angry, anxious, overwhelmed, neutral, lonely, hurt).

_____
_____
_____
_____

What am I noticing in my body? (tension, heaviness, lightness, fatigue)

_____
_____
_____
_____

Set an intention for the day (mind/body/spirit)

_____
_____
_____
_____

How will I practice self-compassion? How will I challenge my inner critic? (I choose to support myself, progress not perfection, it is okay to ask for help, I treat myself as a kind and loving friend, one meal at a time.)

_____
_____
_____
_____

### **Evening Check-In**

What went well today in my healing journey? (I took time for myself. When I ate without distractions, I was able to taste my food. I moved my body). What would I do differently?

_____
_____
_____
_____
_____
_____
_____
_____
_____
_____
_____
_____
_____
_____
_____
_____
_____
_____
_____
_____
_____
_____

*Every day, do something that will inch you closer to a better tomorrow.*
*~Doug Firebaugh*

## Day 6

### Dream
*You can do anything you put your mind to.*
*What is it that you dream of?*

### **Morning Check-In**

How am I feeling? (sad, happy, angry, anxious, overwhelmed, neutral, lonely, hurt).

_____
_____
_____
_____

What am I noticing in my body? (tension, heaviness, lightness, fatigue)

_____
_____
_____
_____

Set an intention for the day (mind/body/spirit)

_____
_____
_____
_____

How will I practice self-compassion? How will I challenge my inner critic? (I choose to support myself, progress not perfection, it is okay to ask for help, I treat myself as a kind and loving friend, one meal at a time.)

_____
_____
_____
_____

### Evening Check-In

What went well today in my healing journey? (I took time for myself. When I ate without distractions, I was able to taste my food. I moved my body). What would I do differently?

_____
_____
_____
_____
_____
_____
_____
_____
_____
_____
_____
_____
_____
_____
_____
_____
_____
_____
_____
_____
_____
_____
_____

*What you practice is what you manifest.*
*~Fay Weldon*

## *Day 7*

### *Listen to Your Body*
*Eat when you are hungry.*
*Sleep when you are tired.*
*Take a break when you need one.*

### **Morning Check-In**

How am I feeling? (sad, happy, angry, anxious, overwhelmed, neutral, lonely, hurt).

_____
_____
_____
_____

What am I noticing in my body? (tension, heaviness, lightness, fatigue)

_____
_____
_____
_____

Set an intention for the day (mind/body/spirit)

_____
_____
_____
_____

How will I practice self-compassion? How will I challenge my inner critic? (I choose to support myself, progress not perfection, it is okay to ask for help, I treat myself as a kind and loving friend, one meal at a time.)

_____
_____
_____
_____

### Evening Check-In

What went well today in my healing journey? (I took time for myself. When I ate without distractions, I was able to taste my food. I moved my body). What would I do differently?

_____
_____
_____
_____
_____
_____
_____
_____
_____
_____
_____
_____
_____
_____
_____
_____
_____
_____
_____
_____
_____
_____
_____
_____

*We have to learn to be our own best friends because we fall too easily into the trap of being our own worst enemies.*
*~Roderick Thorp, Rainbow Drive*

**Weekly Review**

What went well in your healing journey?
_____
_____
_____

Have you noticed any patterns with respect to eating this week? If so, what are they (i.e. eating when stressed, sad, or lonely)?
_____
_____
_____

Take notice of your feelings for the week. What steps have you taken to address those feelings?
_____
_____
_____

What obstacles did you face in your relationship with food?
_____
_____
_____

Were you able to implement self-care and self-compassion?
_____
_____
_____

What are your motivators for creating a healthy relationship with food?
_____
_____
_____

# Week #2
## Identify Emotional Triggers

<u>Lesson</u>:

An emotional trigger is a feeling that serves as a catalyst to overeat. It can be a positive or negative emotion. The first step is to start to recognize what feelings result in overeating. Are there certain emotions that cause you to eat, such as being happy, jealous, or upset? Find out what is driving your cycle of overeating.

*Is it anger?*
Anger at oneself can ignite a feeding frenzy and escalate a vicious cycle of beating up on yourself emotionally (negative self-talk) and physically (overconsumption of calories).

*Is it loneliness?*
Are you using food to avoid being around other people? How might you cultivate a support network? Try volunteer work as a way to step out of your comfort zone.

*Are you tired?*
Studies have shown that not getting enough sleep can lead to overeating. When you are exhausted, the food choices are usually unhealthy.

*Is it boredom?*
Is there a particular time of the day when you experience this feeling? Depending on the time of day, plan an activity that you can do during that time.

*Are you feeling stressed?*
Stress can be described as anything that results in feeling frustrated, anxious, or angry. What might be stressful for one person may not be stressful to

another. Do you have too much on your plate? Take a step back, take a deep breath, and notice the big picture. What can you let go of?

*Self-Reflection:*

Aside from the emotional piece, what are other ways you use food? (i.e., To avoid feelings. As a reward ("I had a hard day, therefore I deserve a treat").)

_____
_____
_____
_____

*Practice*:

Create a coping skills for each emotion listed.
When I am feeling angry I can
When I am feeling lonely I can
When I am tired I can
When I am bored I can
When I am feeling stressed I can

_____
_____
_____
_____
_____
_____
_____
_____
_____
_____
_____
_____
_____

## *Day 8*

### *Motivation*
*We all have good days and bad days.*
*Setbacks are a learning opportunity.*
*Check in with yourself.*
*Are your goals realistic?*

### **Morning Check-In**

How am I feeling? (sad, happy, angry, anxious, overwhelmed, neutral, lonely, hurt).

_____
_____
_____

What am I noticing in my body? (tension, heaviness, lightness, fatigue)

_____
_____
_____

Set an intention for the day (mind/body/spirit)

_____
_____
_____

How will I practice self-compassion? How will I challenge my inner critic? (I choose to support myself, progress not perfection, it is okay to ask for help, I treat myself as a kind and loving friend, one meal at a time.)

_____
_____
_____

## Evening Check-In

What went well today in my healing journey? (I took time for myself. When I ate without distractions, I was able to taste my food. I moved my body). What would I do differently?

_____
_____
_____
_____
_____
_____
_____
_____
_____
_____
_____
_____
_____
_____
_____
_____
_____
_____
_____
_____
_____
_____
_____
_____

*You have been criticizing yourself for years, and it hasn't worked.*
*Try approving of yourself and see what happens.*
*~Louise L. Hay*

## *Day 9*

### *Change*
*Change takes time.*
*Begin to look at the big picture.*

## **Morning Check-In**

How am I feeling? (sad, happy, angry, anxious, overwhelmed, neutral, lonely, hurt).

_____
_____
_____
_____

What am I noticing in my body? (tension, heaviness, lightness, fatigue)

_____
_____
_____
_____

Set an intention for the day (mind/body/spirit)

_____
_____
_____
_____

How will I practice self-compassion? How will I challenge my inner critic? (I choose to support myself, progress not perfection, it is okay to ask for help, I treat myself as a kind and loving friend, one meal at a time.)

_____
_____
_____
_____

**Evening Check-In**

What went well today in my healing journey? (I took time for myself. When I ate without distractions, I was able to taste my food. I moved my body). What would I do differently?

___

*Only as high as I reach can I grow,*
*Only as far as I seek can I go,*
*Only as deep as I look can I see,*
*Only as much as I dream can I be.*
*~Karen Ravn*

## _Day 10_

### *Cherish*

*Cherish who you are as a person.*
*You are special, you are unique.*
*Pay attention to the things that you love about yourself.*

### **Morning Check-In**

How am I feeling? (sad, happy, angry, anxious, overwhelmed, neutral, lonely, hurt).

_____
_____
_____
_____

What am I noticing in my body? (tension, heaviness, lightness, fatigue)

_____
_____
_____
_____

Set an intention for the day (mind/body/spirit)

_____
_____
_____
_____

How will I practice self-compassion? How will I challenge my inner critic? (I choose to support myself, progress not perfection, it is okay to ask for help, I treat myself as a kind and loving friend, one meal at a time.)

_____
_____
_____
_____

## Evening Check-In

What went well today in my healing journey? (I took time for myself. When I ate without distractions, I was able to taste my food. I moved my body). What would I do differently?

_____
_____
_____
_____
_____
_____
_____
_____
_____
_____
_____
_____
_____
_____
_____
_____
_____
_____
_____
_____
_____
_____
_____
_____

*The thing you're claiming has a way of reaching back and claiming you.*
~A.L. Kitselman

## Day 11

*Patience*
*Be patient with yourself.*
*It is okay to stumble.*

### Morning Check-In

How am I feeling? (sad, happy, angry, anxious, overwhelmed, neutral, lonely, hurt).

_____
_____
_____

What am I noticing in my body? (tension, heaviness, lightness, fatigue)

_____
_____
_____

Set an intention for the day (mind/body/spirit)

_____
_____
_____

How will I practice self-compassion? How will I challenge my inner critic? (I choose to support myself, progress not perfection, it is okay to ask for help, I treat myself as a kind and loving friend, one meal at a time.)

_____
_____
_____

## **Evening Check-In**

What went well today in my healing journey? (I took time for myself. When I ate without distractions, I was able to taste my food. I moved my body). What would I do differently?

_____
_____
_____
_____
_____
_____
_____
_____
_____
_____
_____
_____
_____
_____
_____
_____
_____
_____
_____
_____
_____
_____
_____
_____

*You don't have to get it perfect—you just have to get it going.*
*Babies don't walk the first time they try, but eventually they do.*
*~Mark Victor Hansen*

## *Day 12*

### *Solutions*
*Think solutions to your obstacles.*
*Plan meals for the week.*
*Create your own self-care kit and use it in a time of need.*

### **Morning Check-In**

How am I feeling? (sad, happy, angry, anxious, overwhelmed, neutral, lonely, hurt).

_____
_____
_____
_____

What am I noticing in my body? (tension, heaviness, lightness, fatigue)

_____
_____
_____
_____

Set an intention for the day (mind/body/spirit)

_____
_____
_____
_____

How will I practice self-compassion? How will I challenge my inner critic? (I choose to support myself, progress not perfection, it is okay to ask for help, I treat myself as a kind and loving friend, one meal at a time.)

_____
_____
_____
_____

## Evening Check-In

What went well today in my healing journey? (I took time for myself. When I ate without distractions, I was able to taste my food. I moved my body). What would I do differently?

_____
_____
_____
_____
_____
_____
_____
_____
_____
_____
_____
_____
_____
_____
_____
_____
_____
_____
_____
_____
_____
_____
_____
_____

*Whether you think you can or think you can't—you are right.*
*~Henry Ford*

### *Day 13*

#### *Balance*

*Diets don't work; they set us up for defeat.*
*The best prescription is watching portion sizes,*
*moving your body, and eating a variety of foods.*
*There are no good or bad foods.*
*There is room for all foods in a healthy lifestyle.*

## Morning Check-In

How am I feeling? (sad, happy, angry, anxious, overwhelmed, neutral, lonely, hurt).

_____
_____
_____
_____

What am I noticing in my body? (tension, heaviness, lightness, fatigue)

_____
_____
_____
_____

Set an intention for the day (mind/body/spirit)

_____
_____
_____
_____

How will I practice self-compassion? How will I challenge my inner critic? (I choose to support myself, progress not perfection, it is okay to ask for help, I treat myself as a kind and loving friend, one meal at a time.)

_____
_____
_____
_____

### Evening Check-In

What went well today in my healing journey? (I took time for myself. When I ate without distractions, I was able to taste my food. I moved my body). What would I do differently?

_____
_____
_____
_____
_____
_____
_____
_____
_____
_____
_____
_____
_____
_____
_____
_____
_____
_____
_____
_____
_____
_____
_____
_____

*Don't wait until everything is just right. It will never be perfect.*
*There will always be challenges, obstacles, and less-than-perfect conditions.*
*So what? Get started now.*
*With each step you take, you will grow stronger and stronger, more and more skilled, more and more self-confident and more and more successful.*
*~Mark Victor Hansen*

## _Day 14_

### *Support*
*It is vital to have a support system.*
*What are some ways that you can ask for help?*
*There is no need to do this on your own.*

### **Morning Check-In**

How am I feeling? (sad, happy, angry, anxious, overwhelmed, neutral, lonely, hurt).

_____
_____
_____

What am I noticing in my body? (tension, heaviness, lightness, fatigue)

_____
_____
_____

Set an intention for the day (mind/body/spirit)

_____
_____
_____

How will I practice self-compassion? How will I challenge my inner critic? (I choose to support myself, progress not perfection, it is okay to ask for help, I treat myself as a kind and loving friend, one meal at a time.)

_____
_____
_____

### Evening Check-In

What went well today in my healing journey? (I took time for myself. When I ate without distractions, I was able to taste my food. I moved my body). What would I do differently?

_____
_____
_____
_____
_____
_____
_____
_____
_____
_____
_____
_____
_____
_____
_____
_____
_____
_____
_____
_____
_____
_____
_____
_____
_____

*The healthy and strong individual is the one who asks for help when he needs it. Whether he's got an abscess on his knee or in his soul.*
*~Rona Barrett*

**Weekly Review**

What went well in your healing journey?

_____
_____
_____

Have you noticed any patterns with respect to eating this week? If so, what are they (i.e. eating when stressed, sad, or lonely)?

_____
_____
_____

Take notice of your feelings for the week. What steps have you taken to address those feelings?

_____
_____
_____

What obstacles did you face in your relationship with food?

_____
_____
_____

Were you able to implement self-care and self-compassion?

_____
_____
_____

What are your motivators for creating a healthy relationship with food?

_____
_____
_____

## Week #3
## *Identify Environmental Triggers*

<u>Lesson</u>:

An environmental trigger is a place or situation that serves as a trigger for you to overeat. There are a variety of external cues that can trigger eating. For example, eating may be triggered by:

- ☐ Watching a favorite TV show
- ☐ Socializing with friends
- ☐ Walking past a bakery or ice-cream shop
- ☐ Driving in the car
- ☐ Shopping at the mall
- ☐ Being near vending machines

The important lesson is learning which social or environmental cues seem to encourage undesired eating, and then modifying those cues. This is best described as stimulus control. The more often two things are paired together, the stronger the connection between the two so that, eventually one triggers the other. For example, after repeatedly eating ice cream while watching a favorite TV show, just seeing a commercial for the favorite show may trigger a craving for ice cream.
To overcome mindless eating, dedicate a spot in your home (whether in your kitchen or dining room) as your designated eating spot. This helps to eliminate distractive eating that might occur in front of the television or in the car.

*Self-Reflection:*

What are some of the environmental traps that you fall into?

_____
_____
_____
_____

*Practice:*

Keep a log of all the spots that you are eating that are not a designated eating spot to create a greater awareness of your eating traps.

## Day 15

### *Visualize*
*Visualize where you want to be.*
*What does it look like?*
*What does it feel like?*

## Morning Check-In

How am I feeling? (sad, happy, angry, anxious, overwhelmed, neutral, lonely, hurt).

_____
_____
_____

What am I noticing in my body? (tension, heaviness, lightness, fatigue)

_____
_____
_____

Set an intention for the day (mind/body/spirit)

_____
_____
_____

How will I practice self-compassion? How will I challenge my inner critic? (I choose to support myself, progress not perfection, it is okay to ask for help, I treat myself as a kind and loving friend, one meal at a time.)

_____
_____
_____

## **Evening Check-In**

What went well today in my healing journey? (I took time for myself. When I ate without distractions, I was able to taste my food. I moved my body).What would I do differently?

_____
_____
_____
_____
_____
_____
_____
_____
_____
_____
_____
_____
_____
_____
_____
_____
_____
_____
_____
_____
_____
_____
_____

*When you set an intention, when you commit,*
*the entire universe conspires to make it happen.*
*~Sandy Forster*

## *Day 16*

### *Wants*
*What is it that you want?*
*When someone asks you, start to look within—your opinion matters.*

### **Morning Check-In**

How am I feeling? (sad, happy, angry, anxious, overwhelmed, neutral, lonely, hurt).

_____
_____
_____
_____

What am I noticing in my body? (tension, heaviness, lightness, fatigue)

_____
_____
_____
_____

Set an intention for the day (mind/body/spirit)

_____
_____
_____
_____

How will I practice self-compassion? How will I challenge my inner critic? (I choose to support myself, progress not perfection, it is okay to ask for help, I treat myself as a kind and loving friend, one meal at a time.)

_____
_____
_____
_____

### Evening Check-In

What went well today in my healing journey? (I took time for myself. When I ate without distractions, I was able to taste my food. I moved my body). What would I do differently?

_____
_____
_____
_____
_____
_____
_____
_____
_____
_____
_____
_____
_____
_____
_____
_____
_____
_____
_____
_____
_____
_____
_____

*It does not matter how slowly you go, so long as you do not stop.*
*~Confucius*

## _Day 17_

### *Perseverance*
*Change takes time, patience, and persistence, and I am worth it!*

### **Morning Check-In**

How am I feeling? (sad, happy, angry, anxious, overwhelmed, neutral, lonely, hurt).

_____
_____
_____
_____

What am I noticing in my body? (tension, heaviness, lightness, fatigue)

_____
_____
_____
_____

Set an intention for the day (mind/body/spirit)

_____
_____
_____
_____

How will I practice self-compassion? How will I challenge my inner critic? (I choose to support myself, progress not perfection, it is okay to ask for help, I treat myself as a kind and loving friend, one meal at a time.)

_____
_____
_____
_____

### Evening Check-In

What went well today in my healing journey? (I took time for myself. When I ate without distractions, I was able to taste my food. I moved my body). What would I do differently?

_____
_____
_____
_____
_____
_____
_____
_____
_____
_____
_____
_____
_____
_____
_____
_____
_____
_____
_____
_____
_____
_____
_____

*You will have to fight a battle more than once to win it.*
*~Margaret Thatcher*

## _Day 18_

### _Priority_

_When you put things in front of healing your relationship with food,_
_your ability to heal is stalled._
_Commit to putting energy into this healing journey._

### Morning Check-In

How am I feeling? (sad, happy, angry, anxious, overwhelmed, neutral, lonely, hurt).

_____
_____
_____
_____

What am I noticing in my body? (tension, heaviness, lightness, fatigue)

_____
_____
_____

Set an intention for the day (mind/body/spirit)

_____
_____
_____
_____

How will I practice self-compassion? How will I challenge my inner critic? (I choose to support myself, progress not perfection, it is okay to ask for help, I treat myself as a kind and loving friend, one meal at a time.)

_____
_____
_____
_____

### Evening Check-In

What went well today in my healing journey? (I took time for myself. When I ate without distractions, I was able to taste my food. I moved my body). What would I do differently?

_____
_____
_____
_____
_____
_____
_____
_____
_____
_____
_____
_____
_____
_____
_____
_____
_____
_____
_____
_____
_____
_____
_____
_____

*There is a connection between self-nurturing and self-respect.*
*~Julia Cameron*

## *Day 19*

### *Perspective*
*Keep your motivation internally rooted.
When you find that you are focused more on external factors,
take note of that and ask yourself "why?".*

### **Morning Check-In**

How am I feeling? (sad, happy, angry, anxious, overwhelmed, neutral, lonely, hurt).

_____
_____
_____
_____

What am I noticing in my body? (tension, heaviness, lightness, fatigue)

_____
_____
_____
_____

Set an intention for the day (mind/body/spirit)

_____
_____
_____

How will I practice self-compassion? How will I challenge my inner critic? (I choose to support myself, progress not perfection, it is okay to ask for help, I treat myself as a kind and loving friend, one meal at a time.)

_____
_____
_____
_____

### Evening Check-In

What went well today in my healing journey? (I took time for myself. When I ate without distractions, I was able to taste my food. I moved my body). What would I do differently?

_____
_____
_____
_____
_____
_____
_____
_____
_____
_____
_____
_____
_____
_____
_____
_____
_____
_____
_____
_____
_____
_____
_____
_____
_____

*You've got to say, "I think that if I keep working at this and want it badly enough, I can have it." It's called perseverance.*
*~Lee Iacocca*

## _Day 20_

### *Serenity*
*You don't have to make all the changes at once.*
*Choose one practice at a time.*

### **Morning Check-In**

How am I feeling? (sad, happy, angry, anxious, overwhelmed, neutral, lonely, hurt).

_____
_____
_____
_____

What am I noticing in my body? (tension, heaviness, lightness, fatigue)

_____
_____
_____
_____

Set an intention for the day (mind/body/spirit)

_____
_____
_____
_____

How will I practice self-compassion? How will I challenge my inner critic? (I choose to support myself, progress not perfection, it is okay to ask for help, I treat myself as a kind and loving friend, one meal at a time.)

_____
_____
_____
_____

## Evening Check-In

What went well today in my healing journey? (I took time for myself. When I ate without distractions, I was able to taste my food. I moved my body). What would I do differently?

_____
_____
_____
_____
_____
_____
_____
_____
_____
_____
_____
_____
_____
_____
_____
_____
_____
_____
_____
_____
_____
_____
_____
_____

*What we think determines what happens to us,*
*so if we want to change our lives, we need to stretch our minds.*
*~Wayne Dyer*

## *Day 21*

### *Attitude*
*What do you choose to focus on?*
*Your attitude significantly impacts the healing process.*
*Choose to focus on what is going well.*

### **Morning Check-In**

How am I feeling? (sad, happy, angry, anxious, overwhelmed, neutral, lonely, hurt).

_____
_____
_____

What am I noticing in my body? (tension, heaviness, lightness, fatigue)

_____
_____
_____

Set an intention for the day (mind/body/spirit)

_____
_____
_____

How will I practice self-compassion? How will I challenge my inner critic? (I choose to support myself, progress not perfection, it is okay to ask for help, I treat myself as a kind and loving friend, one meal at a time.)

_____
_____
_____
_____

## **Evening Check-In**

What went well today in my healing journey? (I took time for myself. When I ate without distractions, I was able to taste my food. I moved my body). What would I do differently?

_____
_____
_____
_____
_____
_____
_____
_____
_____
_____
_____
_____
_____
_____
_____
_____
_____
_____
_____
_____
_____
_____
_____
_____
_____

*Develop an attitude of gratitude, and give thanks for everything that happens to you, knowing that every step forward is a step toward achieving something bigger and better than your current situation.*
*~Brian Tracy*

**Weekly Review**

What went well in your healing journey?
_____
_____
_____

Have you noticed any patterns with respect to eating this week? If so, what are they (i.e. eating when stressed, sad, or lonely)?
_____
_____
_____

Take notice of your feelings for the week. What steps have you taken to address those feelings?
_____
_____
_____

What obstacles did you face in your relationship with food?
_____
_____
_____

Were you able to implement self-care and self-compassion?
_____
_____
_____

What are your motivators for creating a healthy relationship with food?
_____
_____
_____

## Week # 4
## *Identify Eating Patterns*

*Lesson:*

A food journal enables you to become aware of what you are putting into your mouth. By monitoring and recording your food consumption, you are acknowledging each time you indulge. Therefore, you can break the cycle of unconscious eating. You are now giving yourself the opportunity to turn unconscious eating into conscious eating. Exploring your pattern of eating will create greater awareness of your eating traps. You may be surprised at what you discover.

In your food journal, include things such as:

- ☐ What time of day is it?
- ☐ What type of meal?
- ☐ What did you eat and how much?
- ☐ What is your initial hunger level? (1–10, 1: ravenous, 10: stuffed)
- ☐ What were you eating?
- ☐ Were you doing anything else while eating?
- ☐ How are you feeling?
- ☐ What is your ending hunger level? Are you eating beyond comfort?

*Self-Reflection:*

What is the most challenging part of the day for you with respect to eating? What preventative measures could you take?

_____
_____
_____
_____

*Practice:*

Practice using a food journal for a week. If tracking every meal feels too overwhelming, then just track the most challenging time of your day. For example, if you tend to overeat at nighttime, just keep a food journal for the evening hours.

## Food Journal

| Time | Type of Meal B/L/D/S (Breakfast, Lunch, Dinner, or Snack) | What did I eat, and how much? | Initial Hunger Level (1–10) | Where was I eating (environment)? Was I doing anything else while I was eating? (i.e. watching TV, standing up) | How am I feeling? | Ending Hunger Level (1–10) |
|---|---|---|---|---|---|---|
|  |  |  |  |  |  |  |
|  |  |  |  |  |  |  |
|  |  |  |  |  |  |  |
|  |  |  |  |  |  |  |
|  |  |  |  |  |  |  |
|  |  |  |  |  |  |  |

## Day 22

### *Breathe*
*Take a deep breath and notice what you feel in your body.*

### **Morning Check-In**

How am I feeling? (sad, happy, angry, anxious, overwhelmed, neutral, lonely, hurt).

_____
_____
_____
_____

What am I noticing in my body? (tension, heaviness, lightness, fatigue)

_____
_____
_____
_____

Set an intention for the day (mind/body/spirit)

_____
_____
_____
_____

How will I practice self-compassion? How will I challenge my inner critic? (I choose to support myself, progress not perfection, it is okay to ask for help, I treat myself as a kind and loving friend, one meal at a time.)

_____
_____
_____
_____

## Evening Check-In

What went well today in my healing journey? (I took time for myself. When I ate without distractions, I was able to taste my food. I moved my body). What would I do differently?

_____

*Be your authentic self. Your authentic self is who you are when you have no fear of judgment, or before the world starts pushing you around and telling you who you're supposed to be. Your fictional self is who you are when you have a social mask on to please everyone else. Give yourself permission to be your authentic self.*

*~Dr. Phil*

## *Day 23*

### *Love*
*Extend the love and energy that you give to others to yourself*

### **Morning Check-In**

How am I feeling? (sad, happy, angry, anxious, overwhelmed, neutral, lonely, hurt).

_____
_____
_____
_____

What am I noticing in my body? (tension, heaviness, lightness, fatigue)

_____
_____
_____
_____

Set an intention for the day (mind/body/spirit)

_____
_____
_____
_____

How will I practice self-compassion? How will I challenge my inner critic? (I choose to support myself, progress not perfection, it is okay to ask for help, I treat myself as a kind and loving friend, one meal at a time.)

_____
_____
_____
_____

### Evening Check-In

What went well today in my healing journey? (I took time for myself. When I ate without distractions, I was able to taste my food. I moved my body). What would I do differently?

_____
_____
_____
_____
_____
_____
_____
_____
_____
_____
_____
_____
_____
_____
_____
_____
_____
_____
_____
_____
_____
_____
_____
_____

*Being authentic is the ability to be true to oneself.*
*Living an authentic life requires the ability to be true to our own wants, needs,*
*and desires and not live our lives by the opinion of others.*
*Being authentic is the ability to make self-honoring choices*
*and stand firmly in who we are in our core.*
*~Victoria J. Reynolds*

## Day 24

### Laugh
*Bring laughter into your life.*
*Laughter is the best medicine.*

### **Morning Check-In**

How am I feeling? (sad, happy, angry, anxious, overwhelmed, neutral, lonely, hurt).

_____
_____
_____
_____

What am I noticing in my body? (tension, heaviness, lightness, fatigue)

_____
_____
_____
_____

Set an intention for the day (mind/body/spirit)

_____
_____
_____
_____

How will I practice self-compassion? How will I challenge my inner critic? (I choose to support myself, progress not perfection, it is okay to ask for help, I treat myself as a kind and loving friend, one meal at a time.)

_____
_____
_____
_____

**Evening Check-In**

What went well today in my healing journey? (I took time for myself. When I ate without distractions, I was able to taste my food. I moved my body). What would I do differently?

_____
_____
_____
_____
_____
_____
_____
_____
_____
_____
_____
_____
_____
_____
_____
_____
_____
_____
_____
_____
_____
_____
_____
_____

*Laughter gives us distance.*
*It allows us to step back from an event, deal with it, and then move on.*
*~Bob Newhart*

## _Day 25_

### *Peace*
*Give yourself the gift of quiet time.*

### **Morning Check-In**

How am I feeling? (sad, happy, angry, anxious, overwhelmed, neutral, lonely, hurt).
___
___
___
___

What am I noticing in my body? (tension, heaviness, lightness, fatigue)
___
___
___
___

Set an intention for the day (mind/body/spirit)
___
___
___
___

How will I practice self-compassion? How will I challenge my inner critic? (I choose to support myself, progress not perfection, it is okay to ask for help, I treat myself as a kind and loving friend, one meal at a time.)
___
___
___
___

## **Evening Check-In**

What went well today in my healing journey? (I took time for myself. When I ate without distractions, I was able to taste my food. I moved my body). What would I do differently?

_____
_____
_____
_____
_____
_____
_____
_____
_____
_____
_____
_____
_____
_____
_____
_____
_____
_____
_____
_____
_____
_____
_____

*Learning to live in the present moment is part of the path of joy.*
*~Sarah Ban Breathnach*

## <u>Day 26</u>

### *Relax*
*You deserve some downtime.*
*It is important to have time set aside to recharge and renew*

### **<u>Morning Check-In</u>**

How am I feeling? (sad, happy, angry, anxious, overwhelmed, neutral, lonely, hurt).

_____
_____
_____
_____

What am I noticing in my body? (tension, heaviness, lightness, fatigue)

_____
_____
_____
_____

Set an intention for the day (mind/body/spirit)

_____
_____
_____
_____

How will I practice self-compassion? How will I challenge my inner critic? (I choose to support myself, progress not perfection, it is okay to ask for help, I treat myself as a kind and loving friend, one meal at a time.)

_____
_____
_____
_____

### Evening Check-In

What went well today in my healing journey? (I took time for myself. When I ate without distractions, I was able to taste my food. I moved my body). What would I do differently?

_____
_____
_____
_____
_____
_____
_____
_____
_____
_____
_____
_____
_____
_____
_____
_____
_____
_____
_____
_____
_____
_____
_____

*Don't ever give up.*
*~Origin Unknown*

## *Day 27*

### *Presence*
*Be in the moment.*

### **Morning Check-In**

How am I feeling? (sad, happy, angry, anxious, overwhelmed, neutral, lonely, hurt).

___
___
___
___

What am I noticing in my body? (tension, heaviness, lightness, fatigue)

___
___
___
___

Set an intention for the day (mind/body/spirit)

___
___
___
___

How will I practice self-compassion? How will I challenge my inner critic? (I choose to support myself, progress not perfection, it is okay to ask for help, I treat myself as a kind and loving friend, one meal at a time.)

___
___
___
___

## **Evening Check-In**

What went well today in my healing journey? (I took time for myself. When I ate without distractions, I was able to taste my food. I moved my body). What would I do differently?

*Authenticity is a collection of choices that we have to make every day. It's about the choice to show up and be real. The choice to be honest. The choice to let our true selves be seen.*
*~ Brené Brown, <u>The Gifts of Imperfection</u>*

## *Day 28*

### *Encouragement*
*I am doing the best that I can.*
*What small shift can I make to continue down the path of healing?*

### **Morning Check-In**

How am I feeling? (sad, happy, angry, anxious, overwhelmed, neutral, lonely, hurt).

_____
_____
_____

What am I noticing in my body? (tension, heaviness, lightness, fatigue)

_____
_____
_____

Set an intention for the day (mind/body/spirit)

_____
_____
_____

How will I practice self-compassion? How will I challenge my inner critic? (I choose to support myself, progress not perfection, it is okay to ask for help, I treat myself as a kind and loving friend, one meal at a time.)

_____
_____
_____
_____

**Evening Check-In**

What went well today in my healing journey? (I took time for myself. When I ate without distractions, I was able to taste my food. I moved my body). What would I do differently?

_____
_____
_____
_____
_____
_____
_____
_____
_____
_____
_____
_____
_____
_____
_____
_____
_____
_____
_____
_____
_____
_____
_____
_____

> *If you focus on the possible when you experience difficult situations, you can positively change your outlook, reduce your stress, and concentrate on achieving things that otherwise may not have been possible.*
> ~Catherine Pulsifer

## Weekly Review

What went well in your healing journey?
_____
_____
_____

Have you noticed any patterns with respect to eating this week? If so, what are they (i.e. eating when stressed, sad, or lonely)?
_____
_____
_____

Take notice of your feelings for the week. What steps have you taken to address those feelings?
_____
_____
_____

What obstacles did you face in your relationship with food?
_____
_____
_____

Were you able to implement self-care and self-compassion?
_____
_____
_____

What are your motivators for creating a healthy relationship with food?
_____
_____
_____

## Week # 5
## Utilize Non-Food Coping Skills

*Lesson*:

When you use food as a distraction to deal with the feelings you are experiencing, you never learn to deal with the emotions directly. Food serves as a temporary distraction to avoid uncomfortable emotions. But what happens after the binge? You feel bad about yourself and it creates a vicious cycle of self-abuse. You end up still needing to deal with the original emotion you were experiencing prior to the binge. In addition, there are the negative emotions that come up as a result of the binge (guilt, shame). Breaking the cycle of using food to cope with emotions is a slow and steady process.

Reflect over the past 24 hours. Is there an unresolved issue still on your mind? Once you have identified your feeling, deal with it directly and appropriately. Coping directly with emotions at first will feel difficult and uncomfortable. As you gain more practice, it will be easier and begin to flow effortlessly, but again, not without practice.

*Creating a Coping Box*

To break the cycle, acknowledge the feelings and use a behavior other than eating to deal with those feelings. A non-food coping strategy can be an action, aside from eating, that results in helping you feel better. This is a healthy strategy to deal with uncomfortable emotions. Some examples of healthy coping skills may include going for a walk, watching an uplifting movie, taking a bubble bath, or calling a friend.

A coping box is a collection of your favorite things in one spot. You use it when feeling the urge to binge, or when you are upset, angry, bored, or sad. Place it in a spot where you will see it. For example, if you tend to binge at nighttime, place it on your kitchen table. Supplies needed: Shoebox or a photo box, index cards, magazine clippings, and you can pick and choose the following items to place in the box.

Take into consideration your five senses when putting together your coping box.

- **Sight:** Look at pictures that bring you a sense of calm (old vacation spots).
- **Hearing:** Call a friend. Listen to calming music.
- **Smell:** Light a favorite scented candle. Rub scented hand lotion on your hands. Take a sliced apple, cinnamon sticks, and whole cloves, add two cups of water, and simmer on your stove.
- **Taste:** Enjoy a cup of warm tea or hot chocolate. Mindfully eat your favorite piece of candy.
- **Touch:** Wrap yourself in your favorite blanket. Take a bubble bath. Play with clay.

The goal of trying these different self-soothing skills is to teach yourself how to calm and comfort without the use of food. Add to the list of descriptions the things that appeal to you utilizing sight, hearing, smell, taste, and touch.

- Favorite CD
- Aromatherapy candle
- Bath salts or bubble bath
- Chewing gum or mints
- Favorite movie
- List of friends to call
- Inspirational book or quotes
- Journal
- Favorite affirmations
- Silly putty
- Magazines (that do not make you feel worse after reading them!)
- Craft supplies (colored pencils, crayons, paints)
- Postcards and photographs of places you have traveled to or would like to visit

*Self-Reflection:*

What is the cost of eating to cope with my feelings? Will I feel worse if I choose to cope by eating?

_____
_____
_____
_____

*Practice*:

Create a coping box and make a commitment to use it. What things would you add to your coping box?

_____
_____
_____
_____
_____
_____
_____
_____
_____
_____
_____
_____
_____
_____
_____
_____
_____
_____
_____
_____

## _Day 29_

### *Riding the Wave*
*My coping box helps me ride the wave
when I have urges to binge.*


### **Morning Check-In**

How am I feeling? (sad, happy, angry, anxious, overwhelmed, neutral, lonely, hurt).

_____
_____
_____

What am I noticing in my body? (tension, heaviness, lightness, fatigue)

_____
_____
_____

Set an intention for the day (mind/body/spirit)

_____
_____
_____

How will I practice self-compassion? How will I challenge my inner critic? (I choose to support myself, progress not perfection, it is okay to ask for help, I treat myself as a kind and loving friend, one meal at a time.)

_____
_____
_____

## **Evening Check-In**

What went well today in my healing journey? (I took time for myself. When I ate without distractions, I was able to taste my food. I moved my body).What would I do differently?

*Live with intention. Walk to the edge. Listen hard. Practice wellness.*
*Play with abandon. Laugh. Choose with no regret.*
*Appreciate your friends.*
*Continue to learn.*
*Do what you love. Live as if this is all there is.*
*~Mary Anne Radmacher*

## *Day 30*

### *Self-Care*
*How will you recharge your batteries today?*

**Morning Check-In**

How am I feeling? (sad, happy, angry, anxious, overwhelmed, neutral, lonely, hurt).

_____
_____
_____
_____

What am I noticing in my body? (tension, heaviness, lightness, fatigue)

_____
_____
_____
_____

Set an intention for the day (mind/body/spirit)

_____
_____
_____
_____

How will I practice self-compassion? How will I challenge my inner critic? (I choose to support myself, progress not perfection, it is okay to ask for help, I treat myself as a kind and loving friend, one meal at a time.)

_____
_____
_____
_____

## Evening Check-In

What went well today in my healing journey? (I took time for myself. When I ate without distractions, I was able to taste my food. I moved my body). What would I do differently?

___

*Our best friends and our worst enemies are our thoughts. A thought can do more good than a doctor or banker or a faithful friend. It can also do more harm than a brick.*
*~Dr. Frank Crane*

## *Day 31*

### *Coping Skills*
*Journaling*
*Breathing*
*Calling a friend*

### **Morning Check-In**

How am I feeling? (sad, happy, angry, anxious, overwhelmed, neutral, lonely, hurt).

_____
_____
_____
_____

What am I noticing in my body? (tension, heaviness, lightness, fatigue)

_____
_____
_____
_____

Set an intention for the day (mind/body/spirit)

_____
_____
_____
_____

How will I practice self-compassion? How will I challenge my inner critic? (I choose to support myself, progress not perfection, it is okay to ask for help, I treat myself as a kind and loving friend, one meal at a time.)

_____
_____
_____
_____

## Evening Check-In

What went well today in my healing journey? (I took time for myself. When I ate without distractions, I was able to taste my food. I moved my body). What would I do differently?

_____
_____
_____
_____
_____
_____
_____
_____
_____
_____
_____
_____
_____
_____
_____
_____
_____
_____
_____
_____
_____
_____
_____

*Your breathing is your greatest friend.*
*Return to it in all your troubles and you will find comfort and guidance.*
*~The Teaching of Buddhist Master*

## *Day 32*

***Coping Skills***
*Read*
*Take a bath*
*Paint or draw*

### **Morning Check-In**

How am I feeling? (sad, happy, angry, anxious, overwhelmed, neutral, lonely, hurt).

_____
_____
_____
_____

What am I noticing in my body? (tension, heaviness, lightness, fatigue)

_____
_____
_____
_____

Set an intention for the day (mind/body/spirit)

_____
_____
_____
_____

How will I practice self-compassion? How will I challenge my inner critic? (I choose to support myself, progress not perfection, it is okay to ask for help, I treat myself as a kind and loving friend, one meal at a time.)

_____
_____
_____
_____

### Evening Check-In

What went well today in my healing journey? (I took time for myself. When I ate without distractions, I was able to taste my food. I moved my body). What would I do differently?

_____
_____
_____
_____
_____
_____
_____
_____
_____
_____
_____
_____
_____
_____
_____
_____
_____
_____
_____
_____
_____
_____
_____
_____
_____
_____
_____
_____

*When people believe in themselves they have the first secret of success.*
*~Norman Vincent Peale*

## **_Day 33_**

### *Slow Down*
*You don't have to do it all today.*

### **Morning Check-In**

How am I feeling? (sad, happy, angry, anxious, overwhelmed, neutral, lonely, hurt).

_____
_____
_____
_____

What am I noticing in my body? (tension, heaviness, lightness, fatigue)

_____
_____
_____
_____

Set an intention for the day (mind/body/spirit)

_____
_____
_____
_____

How will I practice self-compassion? How will I challenge my inner critic? (I choose to support myself, progress not perfection, it is okay to ask for help, I treat myself as a kind and loving friend, one meal at a time.)

_____
_____
_____
_____

### Evening Check-In

What went well today in my healing journey? (I took time for myself. When I ate without distractions, I was able to taste my food. I moved my body). What would I do differently?

_____
_____
_____
_____
_____
_____
_____
_____
_____
_____
_____
_____
_____
_____
_____
_____
_____
_____
_____
_____
_____
_____
_____
_____

*Within you right now is the power to do things you never dreamed possible.*
*This power becomes available to you just as soon as*
*you can change your beliefs.*
*~Dr. Maxwell Maltz*

## *Day 34*

### *Notice*
*Notice what is going well in your relationship with food.*
*What small changes have you been able to implement?*

### **Morning Check-In**

How am I feeling? (sad, happy, angry, anxious, overwhelmed, neutral, lonely, hurt).

_____
_____
_____
_____

What am I noticing in my body? (tension, heaviness, lightness, fatigue)

_____
_____
_____
_____

Set an intention for the day (mind/body/spirit)

_____
_____
_____
_____

How will I practice self-compassion? How will I challenge my inner critic? (I choose to support myself, progress not perfection, it is okay to ask for help, I treat myself as a kind and loving friend, one meal at a time.)

_____
_____
_____
_____

### Evening Check-In

What went well today in my healing journey? (I took time for myself. When I ate without distractions, I was able to taste my food. I moved my body). What would I do differently?

_____
_____
_____
_____
_____
_____
_____
_____
_____
_____
_____
_____
_____
_____
_____
_____
_____
_____
_____
_____
_____
_____
_____
_____
_____
_____

*The only people who never fail at anything are those who don't try anything.*
*~Earl Nightingale*

## *Day 35*

### *Ask*
*It is okay to ask for help in this journey.
Who can you invite to be part of your support team?*

### **Morning Check-In**

How am I feeling? (sad, happy, angry, anxious, overwhelmed, neutral, lonely, hurt).

___

What am I noticing in my body? (tension, heaviness, lightness, fatigue)

___

Set an intention for the day (mind/body/spirit)

___

How will I practice self-compassion? How will I challenge my inner critic? (I choose to support myself, progress not perfection, it is okay to ask for help, I treat myself as a kind and loving friend, one meal at a time.)

___

## Evening Check-In

What went well today in my healing journey? (I took time for myself. When I ate without distractions, I was able to taste my food. I moved my body).What would I do differently?

_____
_____
_____
_____
_____
_____
_____
_____
_____
_____
_____
_____
_____
_____
_____
_____
_____
_____
_____
_____
_____
_____
_____
_____

*I define connection as the energy that exists between people when they feel seen, heard, and valued;*
*when they can give and receive without judgment;*
*and when they derive sustenance and strength from the relationship.*
*~Brené Brown*

**Weekly Review**

What went well in your healing journey?
_____
_____
_____

Have you noticed any patterns with respect to eating this week? If so, what are they (i.e. eating when stressed, sad, or lonely)?
_____
_____
_____

Take notice of your feelings for the week. What steps have you taken to address those feelings?
_____
_____
_____

What obstacles did you face in your relationship with food?
_____
_____
_____

Were you able to implement self-care and self-compassion?
_____
_____
_____

What are your motivators for creating a healthy relationship with food?
_____
_____
_____

## *Week # 6*
## *Eat Mindfully*

*Lesson*:

Eating mindfully is being in the present moment with the foods you are consuming. It is eating without distractions and paying attention to the texture and taste of the food you are consuming. Eating mindfully is not as simple as it sounds. What gets in the way may simply be the eating rituals we have established and have yet to break.

When you eat mindlessly, your eating cues can include the sight of food, the smell of food, the sight of someone else eating, or boredom. Creating awareness gives you the tools to break the cycle.

The following four steps outline a plan to turn mindless eating into eating mindfully.

> **Step 1:** Awareness is being in the here and now with food. It is taking notice of when you are eating. Keep track of all the times you catch yourself putting something in your mouth.
> **Step 2:** Check in with your hunger cues. Say out loud to yourself, "Am I really hungry?"
> **Step 3:** Identify the emotion. Ask yourself, "Why am I eating?"
> **Step 4:** Change the behavior. Do an activity that is not conducive to eating.

*Mindful Eating Skills*

- Keep eating contained. Only eat in the kitchen or dining room. Do not bring food into the bedroom or den.
- Sit down when eating.
- Eat without distraction. Turn off the television.

- ☐ Enjoy the experience of eating. Notice the texture, the presentation, and the taste of what you are eating.
- ☐ Slow down your rate of eating. Try putting your fork down between bites.

*Self-Reflection:*

How do I practice being in the present moment when I am eating?

___

*Practice*:

Allot yourself 15 minutes of uninterrupted time for this exercise. Take out two pieces of chocolate.

> *Chocolate # 1:* Go ahead and eat the piece of chocolate as you ordinarily would.
> *Chocolate #2:* Place the chocolate in your mouth and allow it to melt. Notice the texture and taste. Don't rush the experience; instead, be focused in the present situation.

What differences did you notice between the experiences of eating the two chocolates? How might you be more focused in the present with the foods you consume on a daily basis?

___

## Day 36

### Live Slow
*Is there something that you can let go of?*

### **Morning Check-In**

How am I feeling? (sad, happy, angry, anxious, overwhelmed, neutral, lonely, hurt).

_____
_____
_____
_____

What am I noticing in my body? (tension, heaviness, lightness, fatigue)

_____
_____
_____
_____

Set an intention for the day (mind/body/spirit)

_____
_____
_____
_____

How will I practice self-compassion? How will I challenge my inner critic? (I choose to support myself, progress not perfection, it is okay to ask for help, I treat myself as a kind and loving friend, one meal at a time.)

_____
_____
_____
_____

### **Evening Check-In**

What went well today in my healing journey? (I took time for myself. When I ate without distractions, I was able to taste my food. I moved my body). What would I do differently?

_____
_____
_____
_____
_____
_____
_____
_____
_____
_____
_____
_____
_____
_____
_____
_____
_____
_____
_____
_____
_____
_____
_____

*Before you agree to do anything that might add even the smallest amount of stress to your life, ask yourself: What is my truest intention? Give yourself time to let a yes resound within you. When it's right, I guarantee that your entire body will feel it.*
*~Oprah Winfrey*

## *Day 37*

### *Compassion*
*Be kinder to yourself and recognize that change is a process; be patient.*

### **Morning Check-In**

How am I feeling? (sad, happy, angry, anxious, overwhelmed, neutral, lonely, hurt).

___
___
___
___

What am I noticing in my body? (tension, heaviness, lightness, fatigue)

___
___
___
___

Set an intention for the day (mind/body/spirit)

___
___
___
___

How will I practice self-compassion? How will I challenge my inner critic? (I choose to support myself, progress not perfection, it is okay to ask for help, I treat myself as a kind and loving friend, one meal at a time.)

___
___
___
___

### Evening Check-In

What went well today in my healing journey? (I took time for myself. When I ate without distractions, I was able to taste my food. I moved my body). What would I do differently?

_____
_____
_____
_____
_____
_____
_____
_____
_____
_____
_____
_____
_____
_____
_____
_____
_____
_____
_____
_____
_____
_____
_____
_____

*Self-care is never a selfish act—*
*it is simply good stewardship of the only gift I have,*
*the gift I was put on earth to offer to others.*
*~Parker Palmer*

## <u>Day 38</u>

### *Help*
*It is okay to ask for help and support in this journey*

### **Morning Check-In**

How am I feeling? (sad, happy, angry, anxious, overwhelmed, neutral, lonely, hurt).

_____
_____
_____
_____

What am I noticing in my body? (tension, heaviness, lightness, fatigue)

_____
_____
_____
_____

Set an intention for the day (mind/body/spirit)

_____
_____
_____
_____

How will I practice self-compassion? How will I challenge my inner critic? (I choose to support myself, progress not perfection, it is okay to ask for help, I treat myself as a kind and loving friend, one meal at a time.)

_____
_____
_____
_____

### Evening Check-In

What went well today in my healing journey? (I took time for myself. When I ate without distractions, I was able to taste my food. I moved my body).What would I do differently?

_____
_____
_____
_____
_____
_____
_____
_____
_____
_____
_____
_____
_____
_____
_____
_____
_____
_____
_____
_____
_____
_____
_____
_____
_____
_____

*Our greatest glory consists not in never falling,*
*but in rising every time we fall.*
*~Oliver Goldsmith*

## <u>Day 39</u>

### *Deserve*
*I deserve to heal.*

### **Morning Check-In**

How am I feeling? (sad, happy, angry, anxious, overwhelmed, neutral, lonely, hurt).

_____
_____
_____

What am I noticing in my body? (tension, heaviness, lightness, fatigue)

_____
_____
_____

Set an intention for the day (mind/body/spirit)

_____
_____
_____

How will I practice self-compassion? How will I challenge my inner critic? (I choose to support myself, progress not perfection, it is okay to ask for help, I treat myself as a kind and loving friend, one meal at a time.)

_____
_____
_____

**Evening Check-In**

What went well today in my healing journey? (I took time for myself. When I ate without distractions, I was able to taste my food. I moved my body). What would I do differently?

___

*Almost every successful person begins with two beliefs:*
*The future can be better than the present.*
*And I have the power to make it so.*
*~David Brooks*

## Day 40

### *Friendship*
*I am learning to be a friend to myself.*

### Morning Check-In

How am I feeling? (sad, happy, angry, anxious, overwhelmed, neutral, lonely, hurt).

_____
_____
_____

What am I noticing in my body? (tension, heaviness, lightness, fatigue)

_____
_____
_____

Set an intention for the day (mind/body/spirit)

_____
_____
_____

How will I practice self-compassion? How will I challenge my inner critic? (I choose to support myself, progress not perfection, it is okay to ask for help, I treat myself as a kind and loving friend, one meal at a time.)

_____
_____
_____

### **Evening Check-In**

What went well today in my healing journey? (I took time for myself. When I ate without distractions, I was able to taste my food. I moved my body). What would I do differently?

_____
_____
_____
_____
_____
_____
_____
_____
_____
_____
_____
_____
_____
_____
_____
_____
_____
_____
_____
_____
_____
_____
_____
_____
_____

*Getting my lifelong weight struggle under control has come from a process of treating myself as well as I treat others in every way.*
*~Oprah Winfrey*

## *Day 41*

### *Positivity*
*I practice positive self-talk.*

### **Morning Check-In**

How am I feeling? (sad, happy, angry, anxious, overwhelmed, neutral, lonely, hurt).

_____
_____
_____

What am I noticing in my body? (tension, heaviness, lightness, fatigue)

_____
_____
_____

Set an intention for the day (mind/body/spirit)

_____
_____
_____

How will I practice self-compassion? How will I challenge my inner critic? (I choose to support myself, progress not perfection, it is okay to ask for help, I treat myself as a kind and loving friend, one meal at a time.)

_____
_____
_____

### **Evening Check-In**

What went well today in my healing journey? (I took time for myself. When I ate without distractions, I was able to taste my food. I moved my body). What would I do differently?

_____
_____
_____
_____
_____
_____
_____
_____
_____
_____
_____
_____
_____
_____
_____
_____
_____
_____
_____
_____
_____
_____
_____
_____
_____
_____

*All that you do, do with your might; things done by halves are never done right.*
*~Proverb*

## *Day 42*

***Self-Love***
*Do something good for yourself.*

### **Morning Check-In**

How am I feeling? (sad, happy, angry, anxious, overwhelmed, neutral, lonely, hurt).

___
___
___

What am I noticing in my body? (tension, heaviness, lightness, fatigue)

___
___
___

Set an intention for the day (mind/body/spirit)

___
___
___

How will I practice self-compassion? How will I challenge my inner critic? (I choose to support myself, progress not perfection, it is okay to ask for help, I treat myself as a kind and loving friend, one meal at a time.)

___
___
___

### Evening Check-In

What went well today in my healing journey? (I took time for myself. When I ate without distractions, I was able to taste my food. I moved my body). What would I do differently?

_____
_____
_____
_____
_____
_____
_____
_____
_____
_____
_____
_____
_____
_____
_____
_____
_____
_____
_____
_____
_____
_____
_____
_____

*You can be down, you can even be broken, but there's always a way to mend.*
*~Oprah Winfrey*

## Weekly Review

What went well in your healing journey?
_____
_____
_____

Have you noticed any patterns with respect to eating this week? If so, what are they (i.e. eating when stressed, sad, or lonely)?
_____
_____
_____

Take notice of your feelings for the week. What steps have you taken to address those feelings?
_____
_____
_____

What obstacles did you face in your relationship with food?
_____
_____
_____

Were you able to implement self-care and self-compassion?
_____
_____
_____

What are your motivators for creating a healthy relationship with food?
_____
_____
_____

## Week # 7
## Creating Pause

*Lesson:*

When you turn to food when you are experiencing a feeling, you never actually get to deal with what is going on. Food serves as the temporary bandage. Turning to food becomes that automatic response. When you notice the urge to turn to food, take a moment and S.T.O.P. Creating the opportunity to pause creates the space needed to fully understand the feelings propelling the binge behavior. Pause creates a very powerful educational tool for learning about your own patterns of thinking and feeling, and how binging is linked to your feelings.

**S**low down and pause
**T**ake a deep breath *(Practice deep breathing for five breaths.)*
**O**bserve what is going on in your body *(How am I feeling? What am I experiencing in my body? Am I tense? What emotions am I experiencing?)*
**P**ractice doing something different *(What distraction and coping skills can I do in this moment? I can read affirmations, I can use my coping box, go for a walk.)*

Creating pause provides you with the opportunity to interrupt the cycle of turning to food to deal with feelings. It takes you off of autopilot and puts you back in the driver's seat. At first this will be very difficult, but once you begin to use this practice on a regular basis, you will be able to create a new pattern.

*Self-Reflection:*

When have I felt most at home with myself? What steps can I take to make that happen?

_____
_____
_____
_____

*Practice*:

Over this week, take time to stop and check in with yourself. Notice your breath. Notice how you are feeling. Notice what you are thinking. When you have the urge to binge, set a timer and give yourself ten minutes to pause. Using the S.T.O.P. technique outlines above and then check in with yourself by asking the following questions:

*How am I feeling?*
*What is the cost of eating to cope with my feelings?*
*Will I feel worse if I choose to cope by using food?*
*What could I do instead?*
*What do I choose to do?*

## *Day 43*

### *Passion*
*Identify some things that energize and nourish you besides food.*

### **Morning Check-In**

How am I feeling? (sad, happy, angry, anxious, overwhelmed, neutral, lonely, hurt).

_____
_____
_____
_____

What am I noticing in my body? (tension, heaviness, lightness, fatigue)

_____
_____
_____
_____

Set an intention for the day (mind/body/spirit)

_____
_____
_____
_____

How will I practice self-compassion? How will I challenge my inner critic? (I choose to support myself, progress not perfection, it is okay to ask for help, I treat myself as a kind and loving friend, one meal at a time.)

_____
_____
_____
_____

### Evening Check-In

What went well today in my healing journey? (I took time for myself. When I ate without distractions, I was able to taste my food. I moved my body). What would I do differently?

_____
_____
_____
_____
_____
_____
_____
_____
_____
_____
_____
_____
_____
_____
_____
_____
_____
_____
_____
_____
_____
_____
_____

*Be not afraid of growing slowly; be afraid only of standing still.*
*~Chinese proverb*

## *Day 44*

### *Open Your Mind*
*I Wish . . .*
*I Believe . . .*
*I Trust . . .*

### **Morning Check-In**

How am I feeling? (sad, happy, angry, anxious, overwhelmed, neutral, lonely, hurt).

_____
_____
_____
_____

What am I noticing in my body? (tension, heaviness, lightness, fatigue)

_____
_____
_____
_____

Set an intention for the day (mind/body/spirit)

_____
_____
_____
_____

How will I practice self-compassion? How will I challenge my inner critic? (I choose to support myself, progress not perfection, it is okay to ask for help, I treat myself as a kind and loving friend, one meal at a time.)

_____
_____
_____
_____

### Evening Check-In

What went well today in my healing journey? (I took time for myself. When I ate without distractions, I was able to taste my food. I moved my body). What would I do differently?

_____
_____
_____
_____
_____
_____
_____
_____
_____
_____
_____
_____
_____
_____
_____
_____
_____
_____
_____
_____
_____
_____
_____

*Self-trust is the first secret of success.*
*~Ralph Waldo Emerson*

## _Day 45_

### *Determination*
*It is okay to fall down more than once.
I don't let a bad day
define the outcome of my recovery.*

**Morning Check-In**

How am I feeling? (sad, happy, angry, anxious, overwhelmed, neutral, lonely, hurt).

_____
_____
_____
_____

What am I noticing in my body? (tension, heaviness, lightness, fatigue)

_____
_____
_____
_____

Set an intention for the day (mind/body/spirit)

_____
_____
_____
_____

How will I practice self-compassion? How will I challenge my inner critic? (I choose to support myself, progress not perfection, it is okay to ask for help, I treat myself as a kind and loving friend, one meal at a time.)

_____
_____
_____
_____

**Evening Check-In**

What went well today in my healing journey? (I took time for myself. When I ate without distractions, I was able to taste my food. I moved my body). What would I do differently?

_____
_____
_____
_____
_____
_____
_____
_____
_____
_____
_____
_____
_____
_____
_____
_____
_____
_____
_____
_____
_____
_____
_____
_____
_____
_____
_____

*As a single footstep will not make a path on the earth, so a single thought will not make a pathway in the mind. To make a deep physical path, we walk again and again. To make a deep mental path, we must think over and over the kind of thoughts we wish to dominate our lives.*
*~Henry David Thoreau*

## *Day 46*

### *You Are More than Just a Number*
*I am not defined by my body size.*

### **Morning Check-In**

How am I feeling? (sad, happy, angry, anxious, overwhelmed, neutral, lonely, hurt).

_____
_____
_____
_____

What am I noticing in my body? (tension, heaviness, lightness, fatigue)

_____
_____
_____
_____

Set an intention for the day (mind/body/spirit)

_____
_____
_____
_____

How will I practice self-compassion? How will I challenge my inner critic? (I choose to support myself, progress not perfection, it is okay to ask for help, I treat myself as a kind and loving friend, one meal at a time.)

_____
_____
_____
_____

**Evening Check-In**

What went well today in my healing journey? (I took time for myself. When I ate without distractions, I was able to taste my food. I moved my body). What would I do differently?

_Self-esteem is practicing self-care; accepting myself instead of comparing myself to others or criticizing myself and my dreams; being patient with myself and accepting that my mistakes are okay and do not define me; liking myself and viewing myself as worthwhile; and feeling confident to make decisions,
expand my comfort zone, and share my vulnerabilities._
~One person's perspective

## <u>Day 47</u>

### *Believe*
*I find the inner strength and courage
to believe in myself.*

### **Morning Check-In**

How am I feeling? (sad, happy, angry, anxious, overwhelmed, neutral, lonely, hurt).

_____
_____
_____
_____

What am I noticing in my body? (tension, heaviness, lightness, fatigue)

_____
_____
_____
_____

Set an intention for the day (mind/body/spirit)

_____
_____
_____
_____

How will I practice self-compassion? How will I challenge my inner critic? (I choose to support myself, progress not perfection, it is okay to ask for help, I treat myself as a kind and loving friend, one meal at a time.)

_____
_____
_____
_____

## **Evening Check-In**

What went well today in my healing journey? (I took time for myself. When I ate without distractions, I was able to taste my food. I moved my body). What would I do differently?

_____
_____
_____
_____
_____
_____
_____
_____
_____
_____
_____
_____
_____
_____
_____
_____
_____
_____
_____
_____
_____
_____

*Believe in your dreams and they may come true;*
*believe in yourself and they will come true.*
*~Anonymous*

## *Day 48*

### *Encouragement*
*I am doing the best that I can.*
*What small shift can I make to continue down the path of healing?*

### **Morning Check-In**

How am I feeling? (sad, happy, angry, anxious, overwhelmed, neutral, lonely, hurt).

_____
_____
_____
_____

What am I noticing in my body? (tension, heaviness, lightness, fatigue)

_____
_____
_____
_____

Set an intention for the day (mind/body/spirit)

_____
_____
_____

How will I practice self-compassion? How will I challenge my inner critic? (I choose to support myself, progress not perfection, it is okay to ask for help, I treat myself as a kind and loving friend, one meal at a time.)

_____
_____
_____
_____

## Evening Check-In

What went well today in my healing journey? (I took time for myself. When I ate without distractions, I was able to taste my food. I moved my body). What would I do differently?

_____
_____
_____
_____
_____
_____
_____
_____
_____
_____
_____
_____
_____
_____
_____
_____
_____
_____
_____
_____
_____
_____
_____
_____
_____

*If you focus on the possible when you experience difficult situations, you can positively change your outlook, reduce your stress, and concentrate on achieving things that otherwise may not have been possible.*
*~Catherine Pulsifer*

## _Day 49_

### *One Meal at a Time*
*Make life improvements incrementally.*
*I embrace recovery one meal at a time.*

### **Morning Check-In**

How am I feeling? (sad, happy, angry, anxious, overwhelmed, neutral, lonely, hurt).

_____
_____
_____
_____

What am I noticing in my body? (tension, heaviness, lightness, fatigue)

_____
_____
_____
_____

Set an intention for the day (mind/body/spirit)

_____
_____
_____
_____

How will I practice self-compassion? How will I challenge my inner critic? (I choose to support myself, progress not perfection, it is okay to ask for help, I treat myself as a kind and loving friend, one meal at a time.)

_____
_____
_____
_____

## Evening Check-In

What went well today in my healing journey? (I took time for myself. When I ate without distractions, I was able to taste my food. I moved my body). What would I do differently?

_____
_____
_____
_____
_____
_____
_____
_____
_____
_____
_____
_____
_____
_____
_____
_____
_____
_____
_____
_____
_____
_____
_____
_____
_____
_____
_____

*Where the determination is, the way can be found.*
*~George S. Clason*

## Weekly Review

What went well in your healing journey?

_____
_____
_____

Have you noticed any patterns with respect to eating this week? If so, what are they (i.e. eating when stressed, sad, or lonely)?

_____
_____
_____

Take notice of your feelings for the week. What steps have you taken to address those feelings?

_____
_____
_____

What obstacles did you face in your relationship with food?

_____
_____
_____

Were you able to implement self-care and self-compassion?

_____
_____
_____

What are your motivators for creating a healthy relationship with food?

_____
_____
_____

# Week # 8
## Practice Self-Compassion

*Lesson:*

Self-compassion is at the core of healing from binge eating. It is time to disconnect from that critical voice that berates you when things don't go well. Being a kind and loving friend to yourself is a vital ingredient in healing your relationship with food. Would you ever talk to a child, a friend, a family member, or even a stranger the way that you speak to yourself? What gives you the right to treat yourself badly? You deserve to treat yourself with kindness. You deserve to be your own personal cheerleader. You deserve to heal.

A component of practicing self-compassion is to get acquainted with yourself. Imagine meeting yourself for the first time. What are you passionate about? What do you love to spend time doing? What makes your heart and soul sing? What are your values? What things are important to you?

*Self-Reflection:*

How will you practice self-compassion today?

_____
_____
_____
_____
_____
_____

*Practice*:

Schedule a date with yourself this week. Take yourself to a movie, out to lunch, for coffee, to a museum, or do any number of activities that you have been yearning to do, but have been putting off. Take this time to spend some quiet time with yourself. Treat yourself like a new best friend. Come up with a list of twenty things you have been wanting to do, or places you have wanted to visit, and then choose one each week to go to for your date with yourself. I invite you to make this a weekly practice.

## *Day 50*

### *Intention*
*A year from now, I will be . . .*
*Create an intention for where you want to be one year from now.*

### **Morning Check-In**

How am I feeling? (sad, happy, angry, anxious, overwhelmed, neutral, lonely, hurt).

___
___
___
___

What am I noticing in my body? (tension, heaviness, lightness, fatigue)

___
___
___
___

Set an intention for the day (mind/body/spirit)

___
___
___
___

How will I practice self-compassion? How will I challenge my inner critic? (I choose to support myself, progress not perfection, it is okay to ask for help, I treat myself as a kind and loving friend, one meal at a time.)

___
___
___
___

### Evening Check-In

What went well today in my healing journey? (I took time for myself. When I ate without distractions, I was able to taste my food. I moved my body). What would I do differently?

_____
_____
_____
_____
_____
_____
_____
_____
_____
_____
_____
_____
_____
_____
_____
_____
_____
_____
_____
_____
_____
_____
_____
_____
_____

*Believe it can be done. When you believe something can be done, really believe, your mind will find the ways to do it. Believing a solution paves the way to solution.*
*~Dr. David Schwartz*

## _Day 51_

### *Gratitude*
*What things am I grateful for in my healing journey?*
*Five things I am grateful for right now are . . .*

## Morning Check-In

How am I feeling? (sad, happy, angry, anxious, overwhelmed, neutral, lonely, hurt).

_____
_____
_____
_____

What am I noticing in my body? (tension, heaviness, lightness, fatigue)

_____
_____
_____
_____

Set an intention for the day (mind/body/spirit)

_____
_____
_____
_____

How will I practice self-compassion? How will I challenge my inner critic? (I choose to support myself, progress not perfection, it is okay to ask for help, I treat myself as a kind and loving friend, one meal at a time.)

_____
_____
_____
_____

## Evening Check-In

What went well today in my healing journey? (I took time for myself. When I ate without distractions, I was able to taste my food. I moved my body). What would I do differently?

_____

*Gratitude unlocks the fullness of life. It turns what we have into enough, and more. It turns denial into acceptance, chaos into order, confusion into clarity. . . . It turns problems into gifts, failures into success, the unexpected into perfect timing, and mistakes into important events. Gratitude makes sense of our past, brings peace for today and creates a vision for tomorrow.*
*~Melodie Beattie*

## Day 52

### Self-Acceptance
*I am working toward accepting myself, imperfections and all.*

### Morning Check-In

How am I feeling? (sad, happy, angry, anxious, overwhelmed, neutral, lonely, hurt).

_____
_____
_____

What am I noticing in my body? (tension, heaviness, lightness, fatigue)

_____
_____
_____

Set an intention for the day (mind/body/spirit)

_____
_____
_____

How will I practice self-compassion? How will I challenge my inner critic? (I choose to support myself, progress not perfection, it is okay to ask for help, I treat myself as a kind and loving friend, one meal at a time.)

_____
_____
_____

## **Evening Check-In**

What went well today in my healing journey? (I took time for myself. When I ate without distractions, I was able to taste my food. I moved my body). What would I do differently?

_____
_____
_____
_____
_____
_____
_____
_____
_____
_____
_____
_____
_____
_____
_____
_____
_____
_____
_____
_____
_____
_____
_____
_____
_____
_____
_____

*You must love yourself before you love another.*
*By accepting yourself and fully being what you are,*
*your simple presence can make others happy.*
*~Anonymous*

## Day 53

### Authentic Beauty
*I am beautiful inside and out.*

### **Morning Check-In**

How am I feeling? (sad, happy, angry, anxious, overwhelmed, neutral, lonely, hurt).

_____
_____
_____

What am I noticing in my body? (tension, heaviness, lightness, fatigue)

_____
_____
_____

Set an intention for the day (mind/body/spirit)

_____
_____
_____

How will I practice self-compassion? How will I challenge my inner critic? (I choose to support myself, progress not perfection, it is okay to ask for help, I treat myself as a kind and loving friend, one meal at a time.)

_____
_____
_____
_____

## Evening Check-In

What went well today in my healing journey? (I took time for myself. When I ate without distractions, I was able to taste my food. I moved my body). What would I do differently?

_____
_____
_____
_____
_____
_____
_____
_____
_____
_____
_____
_____
_____
_____
_____
_____
_____
_____
_____
_____
_____
_____
_____
_____

*A strong, positive self-image is the best possible preparation for success.*
~Joyce Brothers

## Day 54

### *Healing*
*I am learning to sit with my feelings.*

### Morning Check-In

How am I feeling? (sad, happy, angry, anxious, overwhelmed, neutral, lonely, hurt).

_____
_____
_____
_____

What am I noticing in my body? (tension, heaviness, lightness, fatigue)

_____
_____
_____
_____

Set an intention for the day (mind/body/spirit)

_____
_____
_____
_____

How will I practice self-compassion? How will I challenge my inner critic? (I choose to support myself, progress not perfection, it is okay to ask for help, I treat myself as a kind and loving friend, one meal at a time.)

_____
_____
_____
_____

### Evening Check-In

What went well today in my healing journey? (I took time for myself. When I ate without distractions, I was able to taste my food. I moved my body). What would I do differently?

_____
_____
_____
_____
_____
_____
_____
_____
_____
_____
_____
_____
_____
_____
_____
_____
_____
_____
_____
_____
_____
_____
_____
_____

*If I have lost confidence in myself, I have the universe against me.*
*~Ralph Waldo Emerson*

## *Day 55*

### *Accepting*
*How will I listen to my body in a
caring and compassionate manner today?*

### Morning Check-In

How am I feeling? (sad, happy, angry, anxious, overwhelmed, neutral, lonely, hurt).

___
___
___
___

What am I noticing in my body? (tension, heaviness, lightness, fatigue)

___
___
___
___

Set an intention for the day (mind/body/spirit)

___
___
___
___

How will I practice self-compassion? How will I challenge my inner critic? (I choose to support myself, progress not perfection, it is okay to ask for help, I treat myself as a kind and loving friend, one meal at a time.)

___
___
___
___

### Evening Check-In

What went well today in my healing journey? (I took time for myself. When I ate without distractions, I was able to taste my food. I moved my body). What would I do differently?

_____
_____
_____
_____
_____
_____
_____
_____
_____
_____
_____
_____
_____
_____
_____
_____
_____
_____
_____
_____
_____
_____
_____
_____
_____

*Act as if it were impossible to fail.*
*~Dorothea Brande*

## Day 56

### *Fortitude*
*Knowing that change is uncomfortable,
what is something I can do to step out of my comfort zone?*

### Morning Check-In

How am I feeling? (sad, happy, angry, anxious, overwhelmed, neutral, lonely, hurt).

_____
_____
_____
_____

What am I noticing in my body? (tension, heaviness, lightness, fatigue)

_____
_____
_____
_____

Set an intention for the day (mind/body/spirit)

_____
_____
_____
_____

How will I practice self-compassion? How will I challenge my inner critic? (I choose to support myself, progress not perfection, it is okay to ask for help, I treat myself as a kind and loving friend, one meal at a time.)

_____
_____
_____
_____

### **Evening Check-In**

What went well today in my healing journey? (I took time for myself. When I ate without distractions, I was able to taste my food. I moved my body). What would I do differently?

_____
_____
_____
_____
_____
_____
_____
_____
_____
_____
_____
_____
_____
_____
_____
_____
_____
_____
_____
_____
_____
_____
_____
_____

*Continuous effort—not strength or intelligence—is the key to unlocking our potential.*
*~Sir Winston Churchill*

**Weekly Review**

What went well in your healing journey?
_____
_____
_____

Have you noticed any patterns with respect to eating this week? If so, what are they (i.e. eating when stressed, sad, or lonely)?
_____
_____
_____

Take notice of your feelings for the week. What steps have you taken to address those feelings?
_____
_____
_____

What obstacles did you face in your relationship with food?
_____
_____
_____

Were you able to implement self-care and self-compassion?
_____
_____
_____

What are your motivators for creating a healthy relationship with food?
_____
_____
_____

# *Tools for Your Healing Journey*

## Changing Your Self Talk

In your healing journey, you will tackle your inner critic. Here are some basic tips to give you an understanding of how you speak to yourself.

- The goal is to learn to talk back to the "I can't."
- The way you think about food, eating, and weight loss affects your behavior and how you feel emotionally.
- Certain ways of thinking make it difficult to maintain a healthy relationship with food.

## Common Sabotaging Thoughts Amongst Binge Eaters

- I must be good all the time and not eat anything "bad."
- If I have cheated, I've blown it, so I might as well continue to cheat for the day/week/month.
- I don't have the time.
- This is too hard.
- Food is the only thing that comforts me.

## Talking Back to Sabotaging Thoughts

- Okay, so I ate something I didn't plan to eat, or I overate—it is not the end of the world. I'll get back on track for the rest of the day.
- One meal at a time.
- I am making the time for self-care because I am worth it.
- I am learning to find other things to comfort me besides food.
- I am learning to sit with my feelings.

## Healthy Affirmations

- It's okay to make mistakes.
- Progress, not perfection.
- I am learning to say no to the things that are not important so that I can say yes to the things that are.
- I cherish who I am as a person. I am special; I am unique. I pay attention to the things that I love about myself. Change is not a process that can occur overnight.
- I believe in my ability to change my relationship with food.
- I cherish the person that I am.

## The Art of Journaling

### Why Journal?

Journaling provides you with the opportunity to connect with your feelings instead of holding your feelings and thoughts. Journaling is the conduit to get the feelings out and slow down and pace your thoughts when they are racing. Journaling creates greater self awareness. Often what gets in the way of journaling is wanting to censor your thoughts. Give yourself permission to put the censoring aside and allow whatever comes up to fill the pages.

### Getting Started
- Set aside about 10–15 minutes.
- Write only for yourself.
- Write quickly, don't erase or cross out words, and don't worry about being grammatically correct.
- There is no right or wrong way to journal.

### Journaling Activities

#### Creating a List

25 things I am most proud of . . .
100 things that make me smile . . .
Obstacles I have overcome . . .

#### Feeling Awareness

How am I feeling?
What brings me joy . . .

#### Sentence Stems

I realize I can choose . . .
One of the ways that I am changing is . . .
What I want . . .
Excuses that I sometimes use . . .
Ways that I sabotage myself . . .
What can I take away so that I can feel more replenished as a person?
Why am I so hard on myself?

## Timelines

- Start with your birth or another significant period of your life, place year dates and put in positive and negative things that you remember from that time. This exercise gives you the chance to see patterns over a lifetime.
  - This is also a helpful technique to explore your relationship with food. For example, noting changes in weight

## Pose a Question and Answer Session

- I feel good about myself when…
- What aspects of my life do I enjoy?
- What am I thinking today? What feeling do I get when I think that thought?

## Journal Prompts for Emotional Eating

- If you could no longer use food as a coping skill, what might you do to practice self-care
- What is your greatest fear with creating a healthy food relationship?
- What am I changing about my relationship with food?
- Excuses that I sometimes use …
- Ways I sabotage myself…

## Hunger Cues

**What is your initial hunger level?**
- Are you eating because you have been prompted by hunger cues or are you eating out of emotional hunger?
- 1–4: eating out of physical hunger
- 6–10: eating out of emotional hunger

---
*Hunger Scale*
1. You are so hungry you feel light-headed and dizzy.
2. You need to eat; you feel irritable and cranky. You feel ravenous.
3. Your stomach is growling.
4. Continued hunger signals.
5. **You feel just right—neither hungry nor full**
6. You are comfortably full, a little full.
7. You feel very full.
8. You feel uncomfortably full.
9. Your stomach is so full that it hurts a little.
10. You've eaten so much you feel stuffed beyond capacity; you feel like you could get sick.

---

If you eat at a 1 or 2 (ravenous), you will tend to overeat. When you are eating at any level below a 5, you are eating out of physical hunger. When you find yourself eating at a 6 or more, you might be eating for emotional reasons. Ask yourself what purpose food is serving you. The art of following hunger cues is a balancing act. It is not allowing yourself to get too hungry or too stuffed. Try eating at a 3 and stopping at a 5.

## Emotional/Mouth Hunger versus Stomach Hunger

| Emotional or Mouth Hunger | Stomach Hunger |
| --- | --- |
| ○ Even after I had a large meal, I still want dessert.<br>○ I have had a tough day; I really want something sweet.<br>○ When I walk into the mall and walk by the bakery, I get hungry. | ○ I often get a knowing feeling in my stomach.<br>○ I feel light-headed if I haven't eaten for a while.<br>○ There is a time every day when I feel hungry. |

## Supportive Statements

*Every little bit does help.*
*If I stick with it, it will make a difference.*
*As I continue this journey, I do feel better.*
*It is temporarily uncomfortable as I begin, but as I continue at this, it will get easier.*
*I am worth taking the time for myself.*
*I choose to move my body to help my breathing, help my stress level,*
*and enhance the quality of my life.*
*I am not in a competition with anyone else.*
*I will not compare myself to others.*
*It doesn't have to be all or nothing.*
*I am approaching this in a new way that encourages me to delve into my underlying feelings*
*and to practice self-compassion.*
*I am learning to heal, and this process takes time.*
*I am learning to trust myself with food and to understand what my triggers are.*
*I am learning to do other things to comfort myself instead of turning to food.*
*I am beginning to accept my body.*
*I am doing the best that I can.*
*I am learning about the underlying pieces that maintain my present relationship with food.*
*I recognize that lifestyle changes do take a lot of work initially,*
*and I am being patient in the process.*
*By taking care of myself, I am showing myself and others that I am important.*
*I am learning to understand that the process of change takes time, and with every step I take,*
*I am working toward healing my relationship with food.*
*I deserve to heal my relationship with food.*

## Healing Affirmations

*I deserve the time and space to heal*
*I am discovering who I am*
*I matter*
*I am enough*
*I am important*
*I cherish the person I am*
*I am practicing patience with myself*
*I deserve happiness*
*I am worthwhile*
*I deserve respect from others and from myself*
*I honor my feelings*
*I deserve a great life*
*I step outside of my comfort zone*
*I have the right to take things slow*
*I have the right to take a break when I need one*
*I have the right to have some quiet in my day*
*I have the right to express my feelings*
*I am inspired*
*I am peaceful*
*I enjoy fulfilling my potential*
*I am good enough*
*I deserve good things*
*I believe in myself*
*I practice self-compassion*
*I listen to my needs*
*I accept myself*
*I am okay just the way I am*
*I am beginning to heal*
*I can handle it*
*I can reach any goal that I set*
*I think and act with confidence*
*I am worthy of love*
*I am capable*
*I can be myself*
*I am okay as I am*
*I can _____*
*I can be _____*
*I am learning to _____*
*I deserve _____*

## Michelle Market, LPC, CEDS

Michelle Market, LPC, CEDS is a Licensed Professional Counselor (LPC) and Certified Eating Disorder Specialist (CEDS). Michelle is dedicated to helping adolescents and adults feel better physically and emotionally through counseling, coaching, and workshops. She has a private practice in Herndon, VA, as well as a virtual practice, and specializes in binge eating, self-esteem, and eating disorders. Her mission is to create and maintain positive change in the lives of her clients.

Michelle began her career in corporate wellness before becoming a Licensed Professional Counselor, Wellness Coach, and speaker. She views the therapeutic and coaching process as a collaborative journey of discovery and growth.

Michelle obtained her Bachelor of Science degree in Human Nutrition and Foods from Virginia Polytechnic Institute and State University in 1995 and a master's degree in Counseling and Development from George Mason University in 2000. A combined background in counseling and nutrition has allowed Michelle to offer a unique wellness approach when working with clients who struggle with their relationship with food.

Michelle speaks to audiences regarding making peace with food, enhancing self-esteem, and implementing self-care. Michelle offers ongoing support groups on emotional eating, eating disorders, and self-esteem. Michelle offers phone retreats for healing from binge eating www.michellemarket.com

For more information on retreats and additional resources for binge eating www.healingforbingeeating.com

Printed in Great Britain
by Amazon.co.uk, Ltd.,
Marston Gate.